The Anglo-Venezuelan Controversy: And The Monroe Doctrine, Statement Of Facts And Memorandum

Edward Rodolph Johnes

In the interest of creating a more extensive selection of rare historical book reprints, we have chosen to reproduce this title even though it may possibly have occasional imperfections such as missing and blurred pages, missing text, poor pictures, markings, dark backgrounds and other reproduction issues beyond our control. Because this work is culturally important, we have made it available as a part of our commitment to protecting, preserving and promoting the world's literature. Thank you for your understanding.

THE

ANGLO-VENEZUELAN CONTROVERSY

AND

THE MONROE DOCTRINE,

STATEMENT OF FACTS.

AND

MEMORANDUM

BY

EDWARD R. JOHNES.

1888.
WILLIAM LOWEY, Printer,
85 Nassau Street,
New York.

FACTS RELATING TO
The Boundary Between Venezuela and British Guiana
AND
A MEMORANDUM THEREON.

In view of the great and widespread interest manifested in the controversy between Venezuela and England it has been thought desirable that an accurate statement be prepared containing the facts of the case together with a digest of the diplomatic correspondence between the two nations and a short memorandum bearing on the subject.

The numbers cited below refer to the pages of a pamphlet containing full and exact copies of the letters and memoranda exchanged between the two nations, printed in 1887, copies of which may be seen at the Venezuela Legation in Washington.

By the treaty of Munster signed in 1648, between Spain and the Netherlands the provinces of Essiquibo, Demerara, Berbice and Surinam were the only provinces left in possession and under the control of the Dutch. (III, 39). The provinces all lie to the east of the Essequibo River which running north and south, forms the natural boundary between Dutch and Spanish Guiana; (Map part I.) By an order of the king of Spain 1768 the boundaries of Guiana were further established and confirmed. In 1791 (III. p. 39) an extradition treaty between Spain and Dutch Guiana mentioned as the Dutch provinces the four above named.

In 1797 when the Dutch in violation of Article 6 of

the Munster Treaty advanced beyond these limits Spain appealed to arms to resist the encroachment. This is referred to by Lord Aberdeen in his note to Mr. Fortique dated March 30, 1844. (p. 39 III.)

Thus it will be seen that the frontiers of Dutch Guiana have for over two centuries been recognized as bounded on the west by the Essequibo.

The force and bearing of this will be readily seen when it is considered that England holds whatever territory she has in Guiana through the Dutch. The treaty of London in 1814 (III. p. 39, 48). gave her title to the Dutch possessions in Guiana and by that treaty she obtained what the Dutch had, and no more.

The annexation of any territory not conveyed to her by the Dutch without the consent of Venezuela can be characterized by no other name than that of robbery.

But it is not necessary for Venezuela to depend upon its legal limitations or the records of history to establish the Essequibo as her boundary line. In 1841 (page 48), Major Schomburgk, the English Commissioner, made surveys in Venezuela and planted posts and other marks of dominion. This caused great excitement in Venezuela and the English Government ordered the removal of these marks with the explanation that they had been placed there as a matter of convenience and not as a sign of empire. In 1844 the plenipotentiary of the Republic opened negotiations for a treaty, basing his claims upon History, Geographical Maps and treaty rights, he proposed the Essequibo as a frontier. In 1844 (III. p. 39, 48) Lord Aberdeen proposed the Morocco River as a boundary, leaving to Venezuela as he then stated the free ownership of the Orinoco and its delta. Thus by a clearly defined offer England limited her claims to a comparatively small tract lying west of the Essequibo. This lies far within the survey of Major Schomburgk (I. map) which was repudiated by the English Government, and very far within the claim now actively asserted to the control of nearly all the southwestern half of the basin of the Orinoco. The recognition on the part of

England of Venezuela's control and ownership of the delta of the Orinoco and of Barima Island, is sufficiently supported by a letter from Robert Kerr Porter, the British *chargè d'affaires*, in 1836. (III. p. 11.) That gentleman, in a letter fully recognizing the sovereignty of Venezuela over Barima Island requested the Venezuela authorities to erect a lighthouse on Barima Point. The only answer which has been offered by England to this clear admission is that of Mr. F. R. St. John, who states that the acts of a plenipotentiary cannot be held binding on his government unless confirmed. The reply of Mr. Diego B. Urbaneja, the Venezuela minister, is that after 50 years of tacit permission it is now too late to attack an agreement which has been effectual for that length of time. To show that England's present claims are the results of late discoveries and interesting developments and not the outcome of ancient rights or unsettled claims, the following quotations are made from the correspondence of Mr. Wilson, the British minister at Caracas to Vincente Lecuna (III. p. 7.) foreign Secretary of the Republic of Venezuela, in November 1850. "The undersigned has also been instructed to call the serious attention of the President and government of Venezuela to this question, and to declare that while on the one hand her Majesty's government have no intention to occupy or encroach upon the territory in dispute, on the other hand they will not see with indifference the aggressions of Venezuela upon that territory."

"The Venezuelan Government in justice to Great Britain cannot mistrust for a moment the sincerity of the formal declaration which is now made in a manner and by the express orders of her Majesty's government —namely, that England herself has no intention to occupy or encroach upon the territory in dispute."

The Venezuelan government refused to accept the Morocco or any line further west than the Essequibo, but from this time seems to have admitted that the territory between the Pomaron or Morocco, which join in emptying into the ocean, and the Essequibo, might be considered as being in dispute, and to this "no man's land," was added the territory between the two forks of the Essequibo. Never, however, did Venezuela cease to assert her rights to even these small and unimportant tracts. Considering that she was just beginning to emerge from a chaos of war and revolution, with finances ruined and population scattered and harassed, it is creditable that she stood so decidedly for her rights against the overwhelming odds of English power.

In 1868 the Governor of Demerara in a decree of the division of registers did not establish a more northerly one than that of Pomeron River (III, p. 39), and it was only in 1886, that annulling that decree by orders of her Majesty's Governor, he established new divisions which reach as far as the Eastern shore of the Amacuro. Never losing sight of the boundary question Venezuela urged a settlement in 1876. After 5 years in September, 1881, Lord Granville presented a new line of demarcation which commenced at a point on the sea coast 29 miles east of the right shore of the River Barima. (III, p. 49.) He added that in this manner he satisfied the reasonable pretensions and claims of Venezuela and ceded to her the so-called Dardanelles of the Orinoco and the complete dominion of its mouth This was approved by Mr. Gladstone, and was about to be carried out when the Tory Ministry came into power. Whereupon acting upon the presumable desire to reestablish a strong foreign policy, they refused to carry out the agreement of their predecessors and the Government at Georgetown continued their encroachments.

On October 13, 1883, under instructions from Lord Granville, the English minister of Caracas expressed a wish to settle the boundary questions between British Guiana and Venezuela, and uniting with them the question of import duties and British claims, affirmed that all these questions should be settled together. (I p. 3.)

To this Rafael Seljas, the Venezuelan Minister of Foreign Affairs, replied stating that his government was desirous of reaching a settlement, but referred to a serious difficulty which existed by reason of the fundamental law of Venezuela, which forbids even by way of indemnity, the alienation of the smallest part of the territory which is under the recognized authority of its government. He further stated that consultation with a number of eminent jurisconsults led to the unvarying conclusion that the River Essequibo was the lawful boundary inherited by the Republic of Venezuela as between it and the colony now belonging to England. It will thus be seen that at the very outset of the present controversy Venezuela insisted upon as her boundary line, the river which it claims is not only the natural but the inherited line of division, and beyond which lies to the westward all the territory recently claimed by Great Britain. So much for the point of controversy in 1883. (I. p. 5, 6.)

The correspondence between the governments from November 19, 1883, to March 29, 1884, relates almost entirely to claims against Venezuela, with an adverse reference to the arbitration of the boundary question by Mr. Mansfield in his letter of the last mentioned date. This plan which was urged by Senor Seijas, and supported by the citation of precedents, Mr. Mansfield states on April 7, 1884, is not regarded with favor by England. On April 9 Mr. Mansfield suggested that the boundary be settled by a treaty. To this the Venezuelan Secretary objected, as contrary to the constitution of the Republic. He further urged arbitration as the only means whereby, without admitting the pretensions of its opponent, each nation might lay aside its independence and invoke the decision of a tribunal specially established to pass upon the question.

Thus far the correspondence was barren of results, as Great Britain refused the arbitration of a friendly power, and Venezuela was unable to enter into a treaty. The correspondence between General Guzman Blanco and Lord Granville, which includes the time from December 24, 1884, to June 22, 1885, contains the arguments of both governments and presents on behalf of

England her constitutional objections to laying the matter before a commission of jurists, as also various drafts and amendments of treaty rights already existing. It also contains drafts of treaties, providing for arbitration based upon the protocol added to the treaty of 1883, between the Queen and the King of Italy, and an agreement was made by Lord Granville to refer the boundary question to arbitration. (II. p. 27.)

In a letter to Sir J. Pauncefote, General Guzman Blanco quotes from a letter of George Bancroft in which the latter states that the United States refused six times the offer of arbitration in a matter of the northwest bonndary of the United States, where the question was of great importance and the right clear. (Part II., p. 35.)

The last cited fact furnished a complete answer to the objections raised by Lord Rosebery that it was contrary to English laws to institute an arbitration where the question was one of territorial limits. Lord Rosebury in July 1886 proposed a frontier west of the Iraini which was refused in part, because it was coupled with a demand for the free navigation of the Orinoco, but principally because of its injustice.

The Marquis of Salisbury at this point took up the correspondence with General Guzman Blanco, and the latter continued to advocate the principle of arbitration. He quoted with effect a speech made by Lord Salisbury, calling for a conscientious adherence to terms made by a previous government and ridiculing the principle of ignoring the acts of one agent so soon as another is appointed. General Guzman Blanco then asked for an application to Venezuela of the principles laid down so ably by the noble lord, and that the agreements made by the Lord Granville should be carried out by his successor.

In the vast amount of correspondence which follows one thing is apparently made clear, and that is that while England insisted upon the last dollar being paid by Venezuela of which is claimed by British subjects, she entirely refused to acknowledge the obligation entered into by Lord Granville on the important questions of arbitration and frontiers., although recognizing and approving the act of Lord Granville relating to the boundary of Afghanistan, where the question was raised by Russia, Lord Rosebury however then took up again the boundary question as a basis for treaty and not for arbitration. Against this, General Blanco protested, renewing his argument in favor of the latter course and appending a memorandum, which set out at length the controversy between the nations and deploring the fact that the difference between them was growing wider every day.

It would seem that much of the difficulty met with in effecting a settlement of the boundary question, arises from its complication with the other question of individual claims for damages or the amount of duties on exports. England of late has refused to consider the boundary question, except in connection with the vast amount of claims just and unjust arising from a hundred sources. It would seem that such issues are improperly joined, and that one should not be allowed to affect the merits or adjudication of another. (See memorandum General Guzman Blanco, 11 p. 64.)

The correspondence which next most appropriately falls under consideration is that showing that the occupation by the British since 1885 of land lying along the Barima, Amacuro and Morojuana rivers. Mr. McTurk, the gentleman who headed the secret expedition this year in the English ship *Lady Longden*, steamed up these rivers and the Orinoco, and in violation of the rights of Venezuela posted notices threatening punishment to all infringing the rights of her Majesty of Great Britain. Mr. McTurk arrested Mr. R. Wells, a Venezuelan officer, on Venezuelan territory, and took him to British Guiana for punishment for what Venezuela claims to be an imaginary crime. Mr. McTurk subsequently notified Mr. Kelly, president of the Manao Company, that whatever he did must be in accordance with English law and subject to English control, and claimed in clear terms territory far beyond the frontier.

The following notice was posted by Mr. McTurk at various points along the Amacuro, Barima, Morajuana and Wain:

"Notice is hereby given that any person infringing the right of her Majesty or acting in contravention of the laws of British Guiana will be prosecuted according to Law."

By Command. FRANCIS VILLIERS.
Acting Government Secretary,
Georgetown, Demerara.

But the assertion of authority and the occupation by the English authorities of territory 200 miles west of the Essequibo and of the small tract in dispute is so frankly admitted by the English authorities at Georgetown that it is useless to introduce the proofs of the fact adduced by the Government of Venezuela. (Pages 76, part 2 pages 21, 30 part 3.)

General Guzman Blanco's next letter demanded from Lord Roseberry the following :—First, the removal of all signs of sovereignty erected in the disputed territory by order of the Governor of British Guiana. Second, the recall of all functionaries and public force which may have been stationed there. Third, satisfactory explanations for the non-fulfillment of the agreement proposed to Venezuela by Great Britain, and for the infraction of the laws of the Republic in regard to ports not open to foreign vessels. Fourth, the annulment of the proceedings against Mr. Robert Wells, his liberty and an indemnity for the damages resulting from his capture, imprisonment, trial and punisnment for the imputation of an act of misdemeanor on Venezuelan territory. Fifth, the complete reestablishment of things to the state in which they were in 1850, in which year the agreement referred to was made and strict orders to the Governor of British Guiana to faithfully observe it, until the two governments arrange the question of the frontier.

The third period of this correspondence embraces the communications between F. R. St. John, Esq., Minister of Caracas, and Diego Urbaneja, the Venezuelan Secretary of Foreign affairs. The correspondence ended in a remonstrance on the part of Venezuela and a reassertion of her claims on the part of England. At last the Veneuelan Government broke off all diplomatic relations with England.

Briefly the matter resolves itself into an effort on the part of British Guiana to occupy and appropriate over sixty thousand square miles of territory, only a small portion of which was ever even in dispute. The repudiation of Major Schomburgk's survey and posts, the letters of Mr. Porter in 1836, relative to the Barima Light, the disavowal of Minister Wilson in 1850, the offers of Lord Aberdeen and the agreements of Lord Granville, all point to the conclusion that at the most the only land which has ever been in question is that between the Essequibo and the Pomaron, and between the forks of the former river.

It is also evident that this last invasion and would be usurpation extends far beyond the points where England repeatedly affirmed that she exercised and intended to exercise no dominion or control.

MEMORANDUM.

These facts seem to indicate a continuation of England's historic policy of territorial aggrandisements. indifferent to the rights of weaker nations. The phrase "boundary question," is familiar to students of English diplomacy and is readily recognized as an euphonism, an excuse for invasion and occupation.

Bound to England though we are, by the community of blood, language and literature, united as we are to her by the bonds of commerce and the similarity of constitution and law, we cannot but admit that in her foreign relations she has been grasping and unjust.

The civilizing influences which follow her conquests may palliate, but cannot vindicate her occupation of

India, and Egypt, and the stretching out her grasping hands over Abyssinia and Afghan. Her conduct towards us from our earliest history, the seizure of our sailors which led to the war of 1812, and the Oregon Boundary dispute, all show that the presumptions of right and justice are all against her.

The policy of England in India has been the constant extension of the frontier, and this is openly stated by the English without apparently the slightest idea of any moral question being involved in such a proposisition. Lord Dufferin has received unstinted praise because as Viceroy he had annexed to England a territory as large as France. Yet pride instead of shame seems to attend such injustice.

There is no pretence of purchase or voluntary cession of this territory, only annexation by force.

In other words robbery vaunts itself as virtue and a sublime indifference to moral rights displays itself in an unblushing adulation of the robber.

The rules of conduct which are without hesitation applied to individuals seems to be regarded as trifles beneath the contempt of nations. The greater the criminal the greater the crime should be the law, but who could enforce it against a sovereign power.

Therefore, when England seizes a vast tract of land against the indignant protest of a weaker nation we may in the light of history safely yield our sympathy to the despoiled and turn a deaf ear to the specious arguments of the despoiler.

If it be said that the United States is no party to this quarrel and has no right to interfere in Venezuela the answer is plain.

The Monroe doctrine is not an idle formula, it expresses a policy, it is supported by a principle. That policy, approved by wisdom, sanctioned by experience, should not be narrowed through fear, or limited by selfishness, but should broaden down from precedent to precedent to its full, complete and logical conclusion.

At the Congress of Verona the question arose whether France was right in interposing to prevent disorders in Spain, and at that time (I quote Woolsey's International Law), the British government, authorized the right to interfere, where the " immediate security or essential interests of one state are seriously endangered by another.

As a result of this discussion in 1823 President Monroe in his annual message used the following language: " That we should consider any attempt on the part of foreign powers to extend their system to any portion of this hemisphere as dangerous to our peace and safety," and again, " that we could not view any interposition for the purpose of oppressing (governments on this side of the Atlantic whose independence we had acknowledged) or controlling in any manner their destiny by any European power, in any other light than as a manifestation of an unfriendly disposition towards the United States."

In another place of the same message, while alluding to the question of boundary on the Pacific between the United States and Russia, the President speaks thus: " The occasion has been judged proper for asserting as a principle in which the rights and interests of the United States are involved, that the American continents by the free and independent condition which they have assumed and maintain, are henceforth not to be considered as subjects for future colonization by any European power."

Dr. Woolsey, continuing this line of argument, quotes President Adams : "The principle first mentioned of resisting attempts to overthrow the liberties of the Spanish Republics was one of most righteous self-defence, and of vital importance. And such it will probably always be regarded, if a similar juncture should arise."

The Monroe doctrine came up again in another shape in 1848. President Polk having announced that the government of Yucatan had offered the dominion over that country to Great Britain, Spain, and the United States, urges on Congress such measures as may prevent it from becoming a colony and a part of the dominions of any European power, which would be, he says, in contravention of the declaration of Mr. Monroe, and which must by no means be allowed.

"The Principle," he adds, "which lies at the bottom of the (President's) recommendation is, that when any power on this continent becomes involved in internal warfare, and the weaker side choses to make application to us for support, we are bound to give them support, for fear the offer of the sovereignty of the country may be made to some other power and accepted."

The following quotations are from the pen of Dr. Woolsey who was one of the Geneva Board of Arbitration and the very apostle of peace. "But to resist attempts of European powers to alter the constitutions of states on this side of the water, is a wise and just opsition to interference.''

"Whatever a nation may lawfully defend for itself, it may defend for another if called on to interpose."

Thus from the lips of three Presidents and on the *dicta* of a great authority on international law, we find the Monroe Doctrine supported and its principles applied.

The end in view is to prevent the extensive ownership of territory on this hemisphere by any foreign nation. With England owning Bermuda, Nassau and Guiana, and having Canada on our North, with a seacoast on two oceans she has the United States at a great disadvantage. We know by experience just what neutral ports are in a time of war. But it is beyond argument, that prosperity and our peace are dependent in great measure upon freedom from the complications that must arise from intimate European relations with this hemisphere, especially when these relations are colored by a different system of government. In short wherever American interests are or may be there must we assert the principle of non-interference by European Powers,

Venezuela is nearer to us to-day than Mexico was fifty years ago.

With the increasing closeness of our communication with all parts of the world it grows smaller every year.

There are many citizens of the United States living in South America or having interests there. Grants have been made by Venezuela to American citizens of land within the limits of the territory seized by England. How shall their rights be protected? We are just about supporting an iniquitous system in Morocco, because we have promised that support to aliens, and shall we turn away indifferently and refuse our countenance to the complaints of our own citizens, our own flesh and blood?

French citizens own the franchise for the railway contemplated between the Orinoco and the interior, and many mines are owned and worked by them This fact strengthens our hands in the contest with England.

The Nicaragua Canal will be built by American enterprise, with American money, and our merchant marine and our navy will in time demand that we control it. Shall we have wars and rumors of war and the vast navy of a land-hungry nation at the very gateway of this avenue of our commerce? Do we not need such aid and allies as the three millions of people of Venezuela can give us?

We have just sent a war vessel to bear to his last resting place the remains of a great Venezuelan, Gen. Paez.

We honor the memory of a great soldier, but we permit the spoliation of the country he loved and fought for.

We are quite willing to do a graceful and courteous action, but are afraid to sustain a principle.

But though territorial aggrandisement on the part of British Guiana is pregnant with danger to us, and though the enforcement of the Monroe doctrine seems the most evident method of asserting the theory of non-interference, there is another principle which includes and controls all utiliarian considerations.

This is the principle of justice. There is not one moral law for the individual and another for the nation. The nation is but an aggregate of many persons recognizing responsibility and acknowledging the difference between right and wrong.

The individnal in the absence of constituted authority is bound to prevent a robbery, or an assault,to maintain the right, to oppose the wrong and to assert with all his power the considerations of justice and humanity.

Unfortunately for civilization and religion a different rule has apparently existed among nations, whose kings and ministers have obeyed only the voice of interest, and the allurements of power. No nation can witness the perpetration of a great wrong and say "it is not our affair."

The law of nations written and unwritten guards and guaranties the liberties and properties of every free and independent state, and it is a sacred duty to observe that law.

When great moral laws are transgressed by nations the whole world suffers, and those who have neglected an evident duty suffers with the guilty.

If England had curbed the ambitions of the First Consul she would not have had to rob the cradle and the grave to fill her shattered regiments in order to defeat the Emperor.

The battle of Lodi permitted, made Waterloo necessary.

The dismemberment of Poland was a crime which stains the history of three nations. Have not Russia and Germany paid dearly for this in wars and rumors of wars? And should not Austria blush for her share in that outrage, thinking of Sobieski, the saviour of Vienna? Have not the histories of Saxony, of Alsace and Lorraine been stained with blood because of the unhallowed thirst of conquest? But all history teems with example of suffering and retribution following close upon the footsteps of unlawful ambition.

We know the character of the aggressor, and the helplessness of the victim; we see that selfish interest and eternal right demands that we, a brave and generous nation should not stand idly by and witness the extinguish ment of a sister republic. Two more strides like the present, and Venezuela will be blotted from the map, the prey of the ancient destroyer and creator of nations.

Let us inquire if such interference as is invoked is sanctioned by precedent.

Without question it is. England herself interfered in behalf of the Netherlands against the cruelty of Spain. In all ages history repeats itself, and when the union of two nations under the same dynasty has been threatened, other nations have always stood ready to prevent. Any apparent exceptions have been usually found where unity of race favored identity of government, What would the United States have done without the recognition and aid of France. Did not England give struggling Greece, the countenance and aid which enabled her to become free? In short we must recognize the fact that where interest leads, justice demands, or humanity pleads, that nations should be and often have been actuated by these motives to perform the same honorable acts as the individual.

The ability and patriotism of General Guzman Blanco were rewarded by the agreement of the Gladstone ministry, which the present English government refuses to carry out. No efforts have been spared to bring about a settlement by arbitration, that idea and principle, which England has so often advocated towards other nations. Mr. Olavarria, the Venezuelan Minister, has agreed upon the terms of a treaty with Mr. Bayard, which bring us into the closest and most friendly relations with his country.

Looking at the history of Europe for the past two centuries it will be observed that nearly every war had its source in the effort of some nation to enlarge its territorial limits, and in the consequent endeavor on the part of another to repel such invasion.

Veiled under the terms of diplomacy, hidden by fortuitous and unimportant issues, the struggle has ever been the same, and Europe has shed her best blood to establish and maintain the balance of power,

Then why should we refuse to recognize the duty and perform a trust. Our power is a sacred trust to be used for good, and we must not put aside that duty because it is unpleasant. The facts are well established and the responsibilities which they have engendered rest fairly upon our shoulders, and cannot be dislodged. Precedent and argument only indicate more clearly the path of duty.

Let us then act.

The Government of France, whose citizens have been despoiled should unite with our government in a note of protest and in a demand for arbitration.

The cause of arbitration needs not to be pleaded. It is the cause of civilization as against barbarism, it is in accord with christianity, it is the doctrine of peace and good will. Arbitration is to the nations a self abnegation, a controlling of anger and the lust of battle. It establishes a court and invokes justice in place of brute force, and the ermine takes the place of the suit of mail. Arbitration is in harmony with our century and with its institutions, the appeal to arms is a relic of the dark ages, when independence was punished by the block, free speech was unknown and religious freedom was stifled in the dungeon. What the duel is to the individual, war is to the nation, and one is no more defensible than the other. The proportions are the same and the bloodshed ruin, misery, and demoralization of war, are as great for the nation as they are for the duelist. As Cervantes "smiled Spain's Chivalry away," so the light of to-day has made the duelist appear a laughing stock or a dangerous madman. So it should be with warring nations, whose victories settle nothing except that one nation can burn more powder and lose more lives than another. It is irrational and wicked, and every arbitration agreed to, or forced upon the world is a step towards a universal harmony. The armies may be still maintained, but only as a kind of international police. The Congress of nations contemplated by the bill recently passed in the Legislature should be an historical event, it should mark an epoch in civilization. To this principle of arbitration we should apply the case of Venezuela, and we should act in accordance with the duty that devolves upon us. Before the world will come to acknowledge arbitration as the necessary termination of all disputes, there must perhaps be wars, but each will mark a step toward an eternal peace.

This demand when seriously made must awaken the conscience of England, which heavy with the devouring of nations, seems to slumber, indifferent to the voice of all save interest.

This does not mean war, nor even a rupture of diplomatic relations between us and our mother country. Neither we nor England could well afford a war, but it may mean reprisals, compared to which the territory occupied in Venezuela would be a paltry gain. The violation by a European power of the territory of a friendly sister republic may well excite our indignation and demand retaliation. More particularly so as the invasion is one contrary to our interests and in defiance of a well settled and grounded policy of our government. Failing to obtain a recognition of our interests, opportunity would not be lacking, and that speedily, of such fair and just reprisals as would make England feel that even if not inclined to support justice from principle she might follow its suggestions from policy. The letters of General Blanco and numerous facts and suggestions from Mr. Olavarria must receive grateful recognition in this statement, of which many of the facts have already been presented by me through the public press. All of which is respectfully submitted,

E. R. JOHNES.
Of Counsel.

New York, April 7th, 1888.

Printed by Libri Plureos GmbH in Hamburg,
Germany